BLACKBURN
TO
HELLIFIELD

John Matthews

Front cover: Often double-headed, the 10.25 Euston to Glasgow service was solely in the hands of no. 50015 on Sunday 14th April 1974. Pictured crossing Whalley Arches, the locomotive that is preserved at the East Lancashire Railway, was numbered D415 until 31st December 1973 and named Valiant *in April 1978. Of interest are the different heights of the arches believed to be a result of very difficult ground conditions when the foundations were laid. (Peter Fitton)*

Back cover: The 1947 Railway Clearing House map.

> ### This album is dedicated to my late wife, Sharon, and all my family.

Published October 2016

ISBN 978 1 908174 95 6

© *Middleton Press, 2016*

Design Cassandra Morgan

Published by
>   *Middleton Press*
>   *Easebourne Lane*
>   *Midhurst*
>   *West Sussex*
>   *GU29 9AZ*
Tel: 01730 813169
Email: info@middletonpress.co.uk
www.middletonpress.co.uk

Printed and bound by CPI Group (UK) Ltd, Croydon, CR0 4YY

INDEX

ACKNOWLEDGEMENTS

I would like to thank all those mentioned in the credits, without whom this book would not have been possible. In addition, I am also grateful to the following for their help over many years: R.M.Casserley, G.Croughton, N.Langridge, T.Mercer, J.Roach, D.Salter, B.Watson, K.Wilkinson, Castle Cement, Lancashire County Council Archives and the staff at Preston BR signing on point.

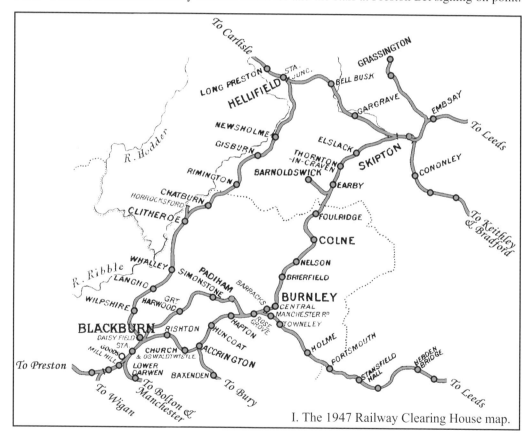

I. The 1947 Railway Clearing House map.

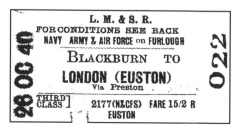

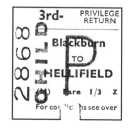

GEOGRAPHICAL SETTING

The Blackburn to Hellifield Railway begins its journey from a highly populated industrial Lancashire town and finishes its journey at the complete opposite, a small, mainly agricultural, village in North Yorkshire. In between, on its 23.45 mile journey northeast, beautiful rolling landscapes are a constant companion as the railway follows the course of the River Ribble, whose name has given the line its nickname 'The Ribble Valley Railway'.

After leaving the Blackburn suburbs of Brownhill and Wilpshire the countryside opens up with great views of Longridge Fell to the left and, ahead, the impressive sloping 1830ft-high Pendle Hill. To emphasise the wonderful scenery along the line, Pendle Hill and a large area north of Clitheroe are part of the Forest of Bowland, an area of outstanding natural beauty. Two more rivers meet the Ribble just north of Whalley, the Calder and the Hodder, that give the town its crest of 'Three Fishes'.

The abundance of limestone around Clitheroe is well known and industries have used it in many ways for centuries. Farmers were early users of the line and, today, huge areas continue to be used for agriculture, as they always were, with Gisburn's weekly cattle market still a regular event. Heading north from Langho, the A59, like the Ribble, is never far away until the railway veers sharply north at Gisburn and the road continues to Skipton. From here rolling fields and farmland take us all the way on the climb to Hellifield.

The maps are to the scale of 25ins to 1 mile, with north at the top, unless otherwise indicated.

HISTORICAL BACKGROUND

In June 1845, the Blackburn, Darwen & Bolton Railway Company (BD&BRC) commenced the building of a new railway with the aim of speeding up the link between Blackburn, Bolton and Manchester, rather than the longer and slower one via Accrington. Along with this, the Company had further plans to construct another railway north from Daisyfield at Blackburn, this being promoted by the Blackburn, Clitheroe & North Western Junction Railway (BC&NWJR). This line was seen as a way of opening up the beautiful countryside of the Ribble Valley to day trippers and

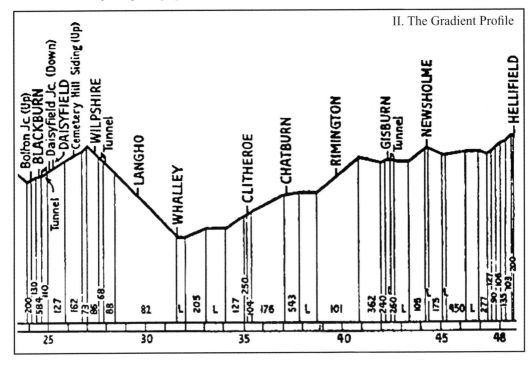

II. The Gradient Profile

also a means for landowners and farmers to move their livestock and produce to the big towns and cities further afield. A link to the then proposed North Western Railway at Long Preston was part of the plans, as was a branch to the lime works at Horrocksford.

At a grand celebration on the 30th December 1846, the first sod was cut by Lord Ribblesdale at Clitheroe and the contractors set about their work. Progress was slow due to a number of issues, one being the perennial shortage of money and the tragedy at Whalley, when three men were killed while working on the viaduct in October 1849. The railway mania of the mid-Victorian times had led to a multitude of small railway companies, many of which struggled to survive. The BD&BRC and the BC&NWJR amalgamated on 9th July 1847 to form the Bolton, Blackburn, Clitheroe & West Yorkshire Railway (BBC&WYR). That was not the end of the change of identity as on 24th July 1851 the Company became simply the Blackburn Railway.

Work continued until finally, on 22nd June 1850, the railway opened to the public between Daisyfield Junction and Chatburn. Even then all did not run to plan as, between Blackburn's Bolton Junction and Daisyfield, the trains had to run over a few hundred yards stretch of the East Lancashire Railway (ELR) and early skirmishes, blockades and tolls charged per passenger made for a far from friendly situation. It was not until about three months into the dispute that a compromise was reached and the hostilities came to an end. The Blackburn Railway soldiered on as a Company for another seven years until 1st January 1858, when it was absorbed jointly into the ELR and Lancashire & Yorkshire Railway (L&YR) who in turn amalgamated on 13th August 1859. Meanwhile, the terminus of the line was still at Chatburn and it brought the Midland Railway's construction of the Settle to Carlisle route to spur the new owners of the line, the L&YR, to start their own work to bridge the gap between Chatburn and Hellifield. This was completed in 1879 and through working from Blackburn to Hellifield began on 1st June 1880. Just prior to the full opening, however, trains had to terminate at Gisburn while the building of Hellifield station was finished. The regular passenger service ceased running on 10th September 1962, but the line remained open, mainly for goods traffic. The full passenger service returned on 30 May 1994 to the southern end of the route as far as Clitheroe, but Daisyfield was not re-opened.

PASSENGER SERVICES

From the full opening in June 1880, connections with Scottish trains using the S&C route were switched from Skipton to Hellifield. Some eight years later it was also agreed that MR locomotives could work passenger trains over the line to Hellifield from Manchester and Liverpool. For a spell, from around 1938, a diesel railcar service operated between Spring Vale (near Darwen) and Clitheroe.

The return of the line's passenger service on 30th May 1994 took a lot of hard work from many people and organisations, including Lancashire County Council, Regional Railways North West and Ribble Valley Rail. The final group mentioned was formed in 1986 with the aim of bringing back passenger services to the Ribble Valley. They continue as a very effective user group and help with the upkeep of the stations. At first there were no Sunday trains, but this was soon rectified when they were added to the hourly timetable from 28th May 1995.

From the late 1970s, regular DalesRail trains have run along the line. These have connected various Lancashire stations like Manchester, Blackpool and Preston, with the Settle – Carlisle railway.

Calderstones Branch

A standard gauge railway from Whalley to Calderstones Hospital was opened for traffic in the spring of 1909 to transport bricks and materials for the building of the hospital. The line from the specially-built Barrow Sidings at Whalley was later used mainly for the inward movement of coal for the power house and heating after the building was complete. Other goods were brought in by rail and oil trains ran for a while as coal was phased out. During the First World War, the hospital was used to care for injured soldiers. This was called Queen Mary's Military Hospital. A tight curve in the line just after Barrow Sidings was a problem for the long ambulance trains and work to correct this commenced in March 1915. By February 1916 there were 1298 patients in residence and, during the Somme Offensive, at least 18 ambulance trains arrived, the first being on 4th July 1916. In the early 1950s, a decision was made to bring in the required fuel and other goods by road and the line officially closed on 30th June 1951.

Horrocksford Branch

The burning of lime around Clitheroe goes back many centuries and, in fact, a byelaw of 1587 states that this should only be carried out by townspeople at a cost of 20 shillings (£1) for every kiln. Pack horses were used to move the lime and it was reported in the 1770s that between 500 and 1,000 loads per day were passing through Clitheroe. The completion of the Leeds & Liverpool Canal in 1816 could have altered the whole landscape of the area, but, after a halt in construction in 1777, the planned route of the canal, via Whalley and Clitheroe, was altered to run near Burnley after the discovery of significant amounts of coal in the area. The Blackburn – Hellifield Railway brought a whole new growth to lime production and in June 1850 a branch line to the Horrocksford Lime Company, sited at the present Castle Cement works, was opened. Further lines and sidings were added to Coplow Hill Lime Works and Isis Cement Works adding up to a very busy scene in those early days. The short branch that climbs away from the junction, initially at 1 in 176 and then 1 in 112, never had a passenger service.

August 1881

July 1910 (Sundays)

MANCHESTER, BLACKBURN, CLITHEROE, CHATBURN, GISBURN, and HELLIFIELD.—Lancashire and Yorkshire.

Miles	Euston Station, 528 London ....dep. 538 " (St. Pan.) "																												
	Manchester (V.).dep.																												
	Salford																												
2½	Pendleton																												
10¾	Bolton (Trin. St.) "																												
13	The Oaks																												
13½	Bromley Cross																												
15	Turton and Edgworth																												
16½	Entwistle																												
19½	Spring Vale																												
22	Darwen																												
22½	Lower Darwen																												
24½	Blackburn 501. { arr.																												
	742,746,783 { dep.																												
25½	Daisy Field																												
27	Wilpshire, for Rib-																												
29½	Langho ....[chester																												
31¾	Whalley																												
33½	Clitheroe																												
37¾	Chatburn																												
39¾	Rimington																												
42½	Gisburn																												
44½	Newsholme [622																												
48½	Hellifield 613, 620, ar																												
125½	620 CARLISLE § ... arr.																												
223½	620 EDINBRO' * .. "																												
241	620 GLASGOW ‡ .. "																												

Down. Week Days—Continued.

(dense timetable data)

NOTES.

a Stops on Tuesdays, Thursdays, and Saturdays.
b Change at Blackburn.
c Arrives at 3 aft. on and after the 11th instant.
d Stop if required to set down from London.
e Except Saturdays.
g Through Carriages, Birmingham to Colne.
h Stops on Tuesdays when required to take up for North of Hellifield.
h Leaves at 10 20 aft. on Saturdays.
k Stops to take up.
l Broad Street.
m Through Carriage, Manchester to Heysham, in connection with Belfast Steamer.
n Arrives at 6 30 aft. on 23rd, 28th, 29th, and 30th instant.
S Saturdays only.
* Waverley Station.
† St. Enoch Station.
§ Citadel Station.

. For SUNDAY TRAINS see page 768.

☞ For **LOCAL TRAINS** and **Intermediate Stations** between Manchester and Bolton, see page 774.

July 1910 (weekdays)

MANCHESTER, BOLTON, BLACKBURN, CLITHEROE and HELLIFIELD

Table 165

Week Days

(dense timetable data)

Week Days—continued / Sundays

(dense timetable data)

Notes.

A Change at Bolton (Trinity Street)
B Station for Ribchester
C Change at Bolton (Trinity St.) Dep 5 minutes earlier on Saturdays
E or **E** Except Saturdays
P Passengers travel via Accrington and change there
S or **S** Saturdays only
⎕ Through Carriages (Table 163)
U from Rochdale (Table 163)

February 1961

SOUTH OF BLACKBURN

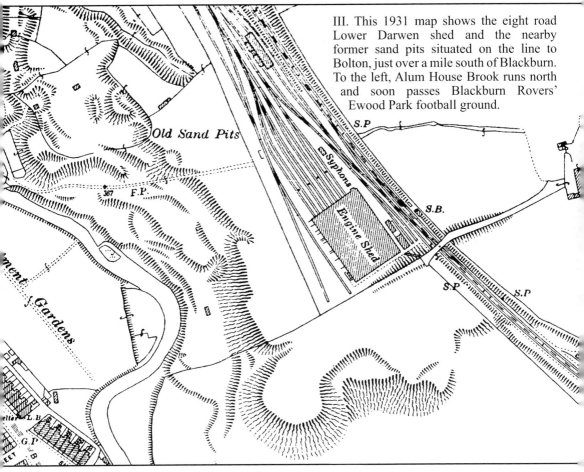

III. This 1931 map shows the eight road Lower Darwen shed and the nearby former sand pits situated on the line to Bolton, just over a mile south of Blackburn. To the left, Alum House Brook runs north and soon passes Blackburn Rovers' Ewood Park football ground.

1. Lower Darwen Shed on 23rd April 1957 is seen with a good line up of locomotives, including a pair of class 5MT 2-6-0 engines nos. 42821 and 42704. Centre stage is an ex-L&Y class 3F 0-6-0 no. 52431, withdrawn in November 1959, and, on the right, a class 4MT 2-6-4T no. 42465. (H.C.Casserley)

2.   Along with Hellifield, Lower Darwen Shed, code 24D, was the home depot for most of the line's motive power. On 11th April 1957, class 4F 0-6-0 no. 43897, a permanent resident at the shed, is ready for the day's work. Built in 1919, it ran until its demise in January 1960. (H.C.Casserley)

3.   We are looking north at the shed here on 11th April 1957. The depot closed its doors for the final time on 24th February 1966. (H.C.Casserley)

BLACKBURN

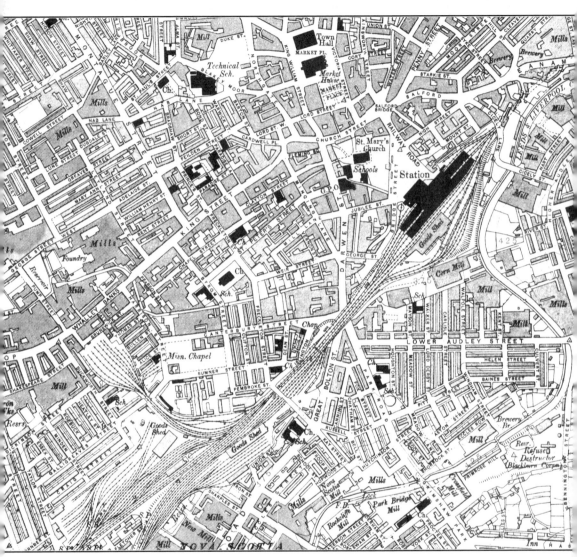

IV.   Blackburn is seen in this 7ins to 1 mile map of 1910 with the station virtually surrounded by mills. The 127 mile Leeds & Liverpool Canal can be clearly picked out to the right. The first barges to reach Blackburn in 1810 brought oil, timber and coal.

Railway Station, Blackburn.

4.   This postcard image shows the station in about 1900. The first station on the present site was opened in 1846 by the Preston & Blackburn Railway. Initially, the BBC&WYR was not allowed to use this station and had to build their own at Bolton Street, a few hundred yards away. That station closed in 1859 and, after some years of wrangles, blockades and amalgamations, things settled down under the L&Y banner. At this time, Blackburn had a population of 127,626 that had shrunk to 104,990 by 1961. (P.Laming coll.)

5.   The Station Square is seen in L&Y days and not a car in sight. Local factory chimneys contrast with the elegant Palace Theatre that had opened on 11th December 1899. After becoming a cinema in 1936 it finally closed in January 1984 with a screening of 'Educating Rita'. (P.Laming coll.)

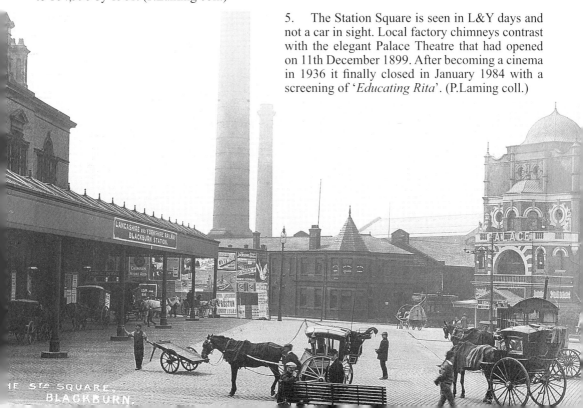

1E STA SQUARE, BLACKBURN.

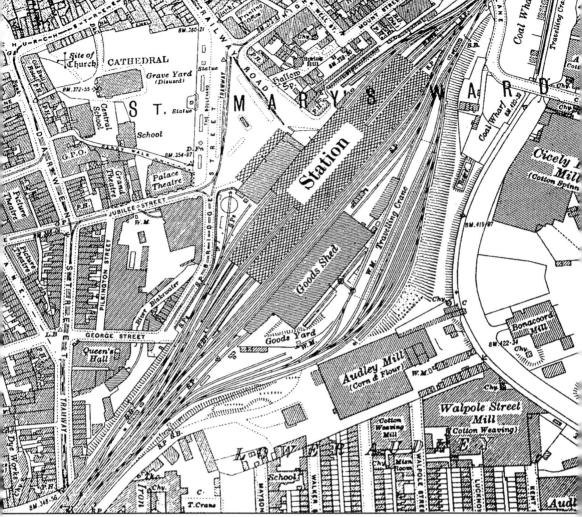

V. The main station and tram terminus in 1931 are shown, with the sidings and travelling crane to the right. Corn, flour, cotton spinning and weaving mills were all well placed to take advantage of the railway. To the left of the station is the turntable, while a little to the north are the Palace Theatre and Cathedral.

6. Moving forward to LMS days, we see the station frontage in 1946. Trams and motor buses have replaced the horses and carts from the L&Y period. Blackburn Corporation did in fact run electric trams from 1899 to 1949. (P.Laming coll.)

7.   Posing for the camera in the sunshine, a trio of passenger guards, still in their LMS uniforms, is seen just after nationalisation around 1949. There had certainly been no rationing when their uniforms were tailored! (B.Howarth coll.)

8.   We look inside the cavernous station in 1954. Standing next to the subway roof, a couple of trackmen and a well dressed 'big wig' inspect ongoing engineering works. They are overlooked by some patient passengers, three large platform clocks and a host of signs and billboards. (K.Roberts)

BLACKBURN.

A telegraph station.

HOTEL.—Bull.

MARKET DAYS.—Wednesday and Saturday.

FAIRS.—Easter Week, from the 1st to 12th May, October 17th.

BANKERS.—Cunliffes, Brooks and Co.; Branch of Manchester and Liverpool District Bank

A borough town in Lancashire (returning two members), on the river Darwen, with a population of 63,126, employed in the cotton trade, Here is a gymnasium, erected by Messrs. Hornby and Kenworthy, for their workpeople. In the 17th century it was noted for its checks (a mixture of linen and cotton), and unbleached " greys ;" but cottons, calicoes, and muslins are now the staple articles. The invention of the spinning jenny, by Hargreaves, who was a carpenter here, and the introduction of cotton printing, by the Peels, have mainly contributed to its improvement. A little cloth is woven. The scenery is flat and uninteresting. *St. Mary's* large parish church was built in 1826, close to the tower of the old building. Queen Elizabeth's Grammar School, at which Bolton, a native, and compiler of the *Liturgy*, was a scholar. *Witton Park*, the seat of J. Fielden, Esq., is near Billinge Hill, 633 feet high, at the end of the Yorkshire hills, whence you get a view of the Cumberland and Welsh mountains, *Stonyhurst*, is a Tudor built College for Roman Catholics, at which 180 students are received.

From Bradshaw's Guide of 1866

9.   At the west end of the station, class 4MT 2-6-4T no. 42666 awaits departure for Wigan on 23rd April 1954. Off to the left is the station turntable, its outline still visible today, over 60 years later. The engine was built in 1942 and had a relatively short life, being withdrawn from Barrow in September 1962. (H.C.Casserley)

10. The SLS 'Northern Dales Railtour' of 4th September 1955 waits at Blackburn on the return leg of the tour back to Manchester. The loco is a class 4P 4-4-0 compound no. 41102 built in 1925. It was withdrawn on the last day of 1958. (H.C.Casserley)

11. This is a view at the east end of the station in 1964. About to head off towards Daisyfield, probably to take up banking duties at Whalley, is Lower Darwen locomotive no. 43019. Note the fish dock to the left. The 59 ton 2-6-0 engine ran for just 20 years, being retired from Lostock Hall in May 1968. (A.Mercer)

12. At the end of steam, one of the many special trains to visit Blackburn was the 'Farewell to Steam 2'. On 4th August 1968, black five class nos 44874 and 45017 take water at the west end of the station. The special had started from Birmingham, taking a grand tour through Manchester, Diggle, Huddersfield and then over Copy Pit. In the distance is the 78-lever West signal box, built in 1904. Both Blackburn East and West boxes closed on 20th August 1972, as part of the Preston resignalling scheme. (G.Turner)

13. A Colne - Preston Cravens DMU arrives with much of the steam age items still in place, although the fish dock to the left is no longer present. The East box and plenty of semaphores were still intact on 11th March 1972. The signal box was an L&Y type with some 80 levers dating from 1903. (P.J.Fitton)

14. High in one of the train shed roofs is the last operational L&Y signal, seen on 11th March 1972. It was pulled off especially for the photographer when the light was just right. (P.J.Fitton)

15. The end is nigh for both the station sign and gas light shortly before being replaced, early in 1972. (P.J.Fitton)

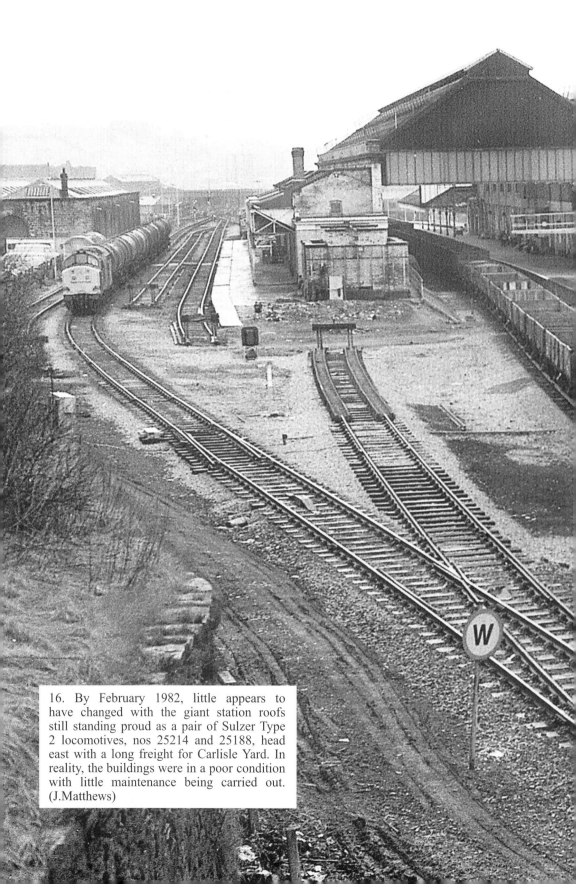

16. By February 1982, little appears to have changed with the giant station roofs still standing proud as a pair of Sulzer Type 2 locomotives, nos 25214 and 25188, head east with a long freight for Carlisle Yard. In reality, the buildings were in a poor condition with little maintenance being carried out. (J.Matthews)

17. By the early 1980s, Bolton Road Goods Yard was the main freight location. On 2nd December 1983, class 47 no. 47368 had arrived with a coal train for the King Street depot, as no. 25256 shunts its train of steel for Fogarty's depot and cement tanks for Clitheroe. A 10-ton crane would have been available for use here in the early LMS days (J.Matthews)

18. With the ending of long distance through freight trains in May 1983, the station's train crew depot closed in December of the same year. The occasional crew change still took place, as witnessed here on 29th April 1984 with the 09.45 Glasgow - Manchester Red Bank empty newspaper vans. The locomotive, no. 40028, had less than six months still in service, seeing the end on 17th October 1984. On the far left is the surviving station clock and below it, an Isle of Man Steam Packet display case complete with model ferry boat. (*J. Matthews*)

3rd-SINGLE   SINGLE-3rd

5054

Wilpshire   Wilpshire
        Wilpshire   To
Blackburn   Blackburn
BLACKBURN

5054

(M) -/6 H   FARE -/6 H (M)

For conditions see over For conditions see over

British Transport Commission (M)

0252

PARKING TICKET FOR MOTOR CAR
OR THREE-WHEELED VEHICLE AT

WILPSHIRE (GOODS)

Registration No.........................

Fee 1/0

Available on Day of Issue only
FOR CONDITIONS SEE OVER

0252

19.   At Bolton Street Yard on 18th February 1987, we see nos 37109 and 37191 running onto an afternoon cement trip for Clitheroe, while in the busy yard a new traffic of Leyland DAF lorries is being loaded for export. Even after the demise of the Speedlink network, this was still a busy place for freight. Over time though, traffic, like coal, steel and chipboard, were lost and the last goods service to date was an occasional stone train running in July 2013. (J.Matthews)

20.   The King Street Coal Yard, or Coal Concentration Depot as it was known in later days, is viewed in October 1998. Long coal trains would arrive from numerous locations, including the South of Scotland, the north-east and the Yorkshire coalfields, with the empty HEA wagons for the north often returning via the Ribble Valley. (J Matthews)

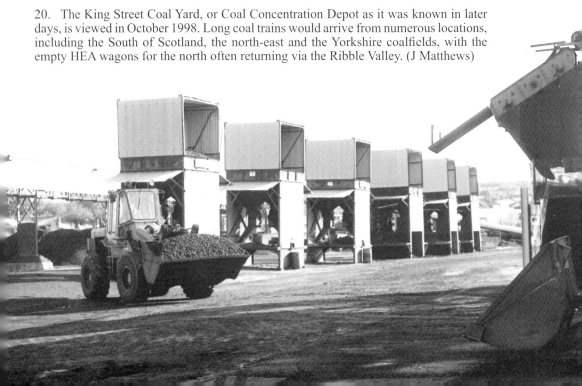

21. The King Street Coal Depot was closed in early 1999, but a few months before closure the yard had employed the services of no. 08578 to shunt the wagons. The diesel shunter, originally D3745, was built at Crewe Works in June 1959 and at the end of 2015 was still alive, albeit stored at Toton. (J.Matthews)

22. Demolishing of the old station is well under way in this view of 30th July 1999. Years of neglect had finally taken its toll with parts of the station being deemed unsafe. Part of the overall roof has already gone as no. 142010 waits with a Colne - Blackpool South service. (J.Matthews)

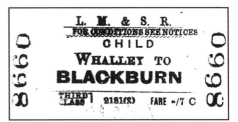

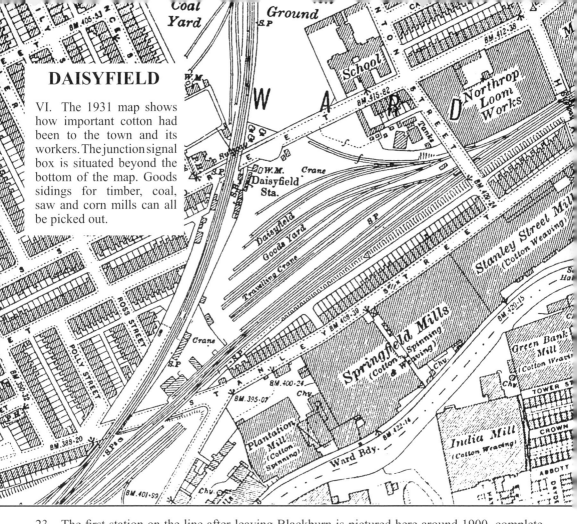

DAISYFIELD

VI. The 1931 map shows how important cotton had been to the town and its workers. The junction signal box is situated beyond the bottom of the map. Goods sidings for timber, coal, saw and corn mills can all be picked out.

23. The first station on the line after leaving Blackburn is pictured here around 1900, complete with signal box, crossing gates and station staff. Opened in 1872, it closed for passengers and goods on 3rd November 1958, some four years before many of the other stations along the route. (P.Laming coll.)

24. Viewed from a Hellifield bound service, we are looking back towards Blackburn's industrial backdrop of mills and chimneys on 23rd April 1954. (H.C.Casserley)

25. There were a host of sidings and goods yards around Daisyfield, one even equipped with a 40-ton crane. Seen here in the late 1950s is the locomotive that once shunted the Appleby Flour Mill sidings, an 1895 0-4-0ST built by Peckett & Sons in 1895. Nicknamed 'Little A' by the locals, it was purchased by the mill in 1906 and worked its grain wagons well into the 1960s. (B.Haworth coll.)

26. This is Moss Street level crossing in 1962 and ex-LMS class 5MT 2-6-0 no. 42755 is heading past the signal box and over the underpass with a northbound freight. The engine, built in 1927, ran another two years or so until October 1964. (K.Roberts)

27. The steam crane is busy at Daisyfield's former platforms on 3rd December 1974, attending to the debris from a freight train derailment. To the left are the remains of a four-wheeled van, while on the up platform stand a couple of covered hoppers looking relatively undamaged. A strong smell of whisky hung over the crash scene. (P.J.Fitton)

28. In June 1980, a wave from the signalman greets the morning loaded ballast train from Ribblehead as it rumbles through the crossing heading for Blackburn. The signal box, still in use in 2016, is a Saxby and Farmer type 6 built in 1873, and is now a Grade II listed building. Originally it had been fitted with a 20-lever S&F frame, but this was replaced by a second-hand 16-lever L&Y type in 1943. (J.Matthews)

29. The mills and factories to the right are no longer served by the railway. We see no. 47524 easing through the points at Daisyfield Junction and on towards Blackburn. The train is the 08:20 Glasgow - Euston diversion pictured on 21st February 1982. Up until September 1973 the junction had its own signal box situated to the left, which dated from the 1880s. (J.Matthews)

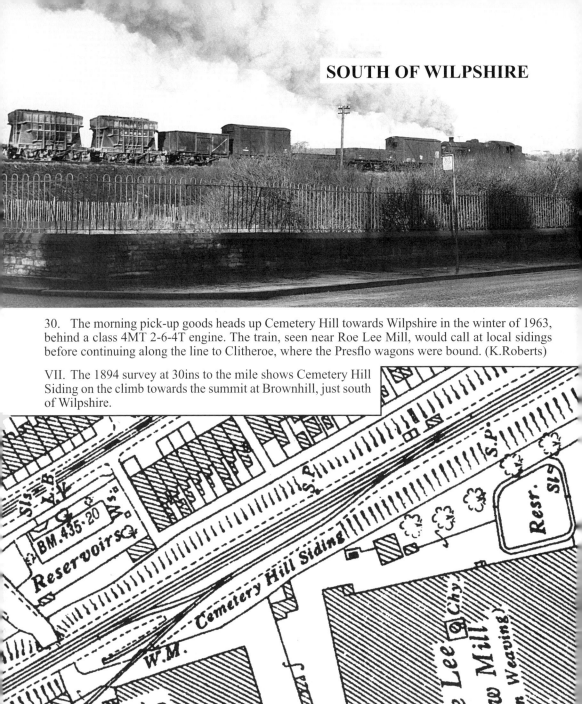

30. The morning pick-up goods heads up Cemetery Hill towards Wilpshire in the winter of 1963, behind a class 4MT 2-6-4T engine. The train, seen near Roe Lee Mill, would call at local sidings before continuing along the line to Clitheroe, where the Presflo wagons were bound. (K.Roberts)

VII. The 1894 survey at 30ins to the mile shows Cemetery Hill Siding on the climb towards the summit at Brownhill, just south of Wilpshire.

31.   Leaving Blackburn behind, we are looking at the fine sight of no. 76084 nearing Brownhill with the 10.19 Blackburn - Hellifield service in January 1959. The Standard class 4 2-6-0, built at Horwich in April 1957, was a Lower Darwen engine before being withdrawn in December 1967. (K.Roberts)

32.   After the 1 in 73 climb out of Blackburn, a Stockport to Carlisle charter train is breasting the summit at Brownhill and nearing Wilpshire behind A1A locomotives no. 31404 and no. 31405 on 15th September 1990. (J.Matthews)

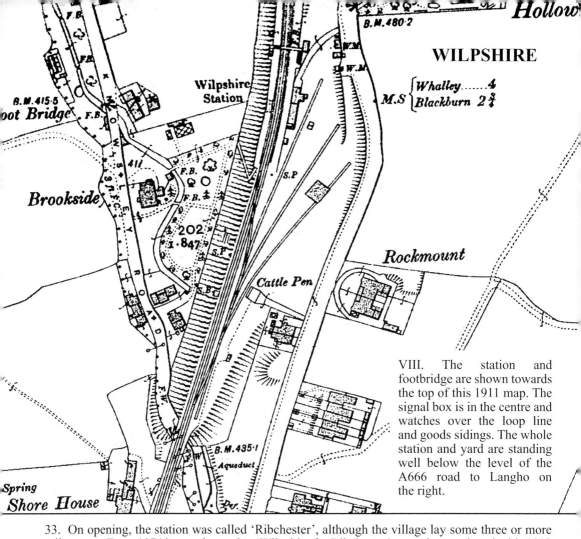

Hollow

WILPSHIRE

$$M.S \begin{cases} \text{Whalley} \dots \dots 4 \\ \text{Blackburn } 2\frac{3}{4} \end{cases}$$

B.M.480.2

B.M.415.5

oot Bridge

Brookside

411

202

1.847

S.P.

Cattle Pen

Rockmount

B.M.435.1

Aqueduct

Spring
Shore House

Wilpshire
Station

VIII. The station and footbridge are shown towards the top of this 1911 map. The signal box is in the centre and watches over the loop line and goods sidings. The whole station and yard are standing well below the level of the A666 road to Langho on the right.

33.   On opening, the station was called 'Ribchester', although the village lay some three or more miles away. From 1874 it was changed to 'Wilpshire for Ribchester' as can be seen here in this 1912 view, as we look towards Clitheroe. Unlike Blackburn, Wilpshire saw an increase in population, from 594 in 1901 to 1451 in 1961. (Lens of Sutton)

34. A 1953 view of the station has the wooden northbound platform still in situ, as no. 44579 heads a train of coal empties towards Blackburn. The class 4F 0-6-0 ended its days at Skipton in October 1962 after being a Hellifield resident. (K.Roberts)

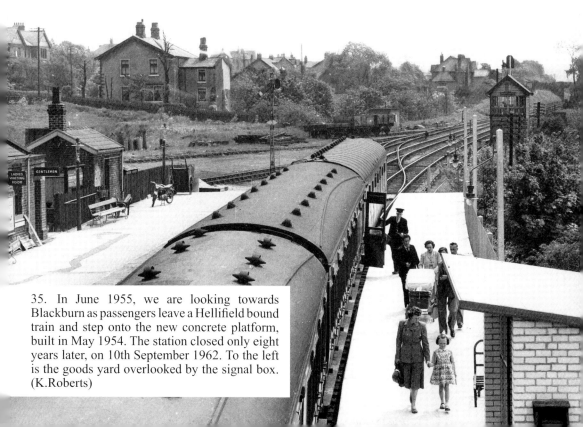

35. In June 1955, we are looking towards Blackburn as passengers leave a Hellifield bound train and step onto the new concrete platform, built in May 1954. The station closed only eight years later, on 10th September 1962. To the left is the goods yard overlooked by the signal box. (K.Roberts)

36.   The goods yard is pictured on a wintry February morning in 1955. There appears to be some coal traffic and, although the yard had a 4-ton crane and handled a variety of goods and livestock, it closed on 2nd November 1964. (K.Roberts)

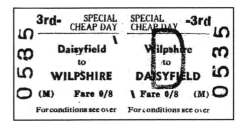

37. In 1963, the signalman poses in his 16-lever frame box, which dated from 1926. The second-hand ex-L&Y top on a brick base had replaced the original one, named Ribchester, built in 1873. It was officially closed on the 18th March 1981, but was out of use for a year or so earlier. (K.Roberts)

38. We now look from the signal box in the summer of 1964 as Standard class 9F no. 92022 brings an up goods train through the station, still with its footbridge in place. The 2-10-0 engine was in traffic for just over 12 years when withdrawn on 30th November 1967 from Birkenhead depot. (K.Roberts)

39.   On 7th July 1980, no. 47187 heads north past the now unmanned box with a down air-braked freight for Mossend Yard. Vegetation is moving in and the box was officially closed some eight months later. (J.Matthews)

L. & N. W. R.
Issued subject to the conditions in the Cos Time Tables Books, Bills & Notices
OUTWARD HALF
THIRD CLASS
WILPSHIRE FOR R.
TO
BLACKBURN
(R)
burn   Fare 9d
8019

3rd-SINGLE   SINGLE-3rd
Langho   Langho
Langho   To
Clitheroe   Clitheroe
CLITHEROE
(M) -/11 H FARE -/11 H (M)
For conditions see over For conditions see over
079   079

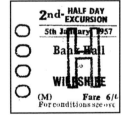

2nd- HALF DAY EXCURSION
5th January 1957
Bank Hall
WILPSHIRE
(M)   Fare 6/t
For conditions see ove

L.M.&S.R. FOR CONDITIONS SEE BACK
SPECIAL DAY EXN
Return as per bill
Steerage & 3rd Class
Douglas (IofM)
TO
LANGHO
Via LMS Dos Steamer
Liverpool & LM&SR
SPECIAL DOUGLAS

L. M. & S. R.
SPECIAL
DAY EXCURSION
3rd Class & Steerage
Langho
TO
DOUGLAS (IofM)
Via LM&SR L'pool(Ex) & IofM.S.P.Co.Steamer to destination
2186 SplD.vL DMSPC
C23   C23

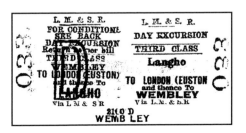

L. M. & S. R.
FOR CONDITIONS SEE BACK
DAY EXCURSION
Return as per bill
THIRD CLASS
WEMBLEY
TO LONDON (EUSTON)
and thence to
LANGHO
Via LM & SR

L. M. & S. R.
DAY EXCURSION
THIRD CLASS
Langho
TO LONDON (EUSTON
and thence To
WEMBLEY
Via LM. & S.R.
2100 D
WEMBLEY
C3   C3

40. Seen climbing Whalley Bank before it passes Wilpshire, locomotive no. 40180 heads towards Blackburn with the empty vans for Red Bank on Sunday 18th April 1982. The station house, looking in a dreadful state, was saved and today is a private residence. (J.Matthews)

41. Amazingly, only seven weeks before the new station opened, a building site greets ex-LNER class A4 locomotive no. 4498 *Sir Nigel Gresley*, here running south for Farington Junction to take over a special charter. The new station is just south of the earlier one, whose station house can be seen in the distance on 9th April 1994. (J.Matthews)

42. The first train to use the line's new station, no. 156427, calls at the spotless renamed Ramsgreave & Wilpshire station. The train in question is the Sundays Only Blackpool North - Carlisle 'DalesRail' seen on 29th May 1994. The new daily passenger service for Langho, Whalley and Clitheroe started the following day. (J.Matthews)

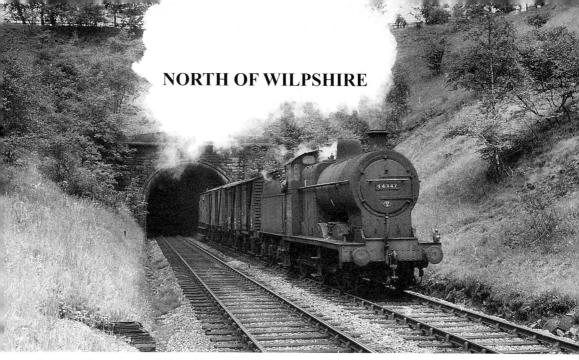

43.   The view here is of class 4F 0-6-0 no. 44347 leaving the 325-yard Wilpshire Tunnel, with a short freight train destined for Blackburn in July 1963. (K.Roberts)

44.   Having left the tunnel behind, no. 40151 passes under the B6245 for Ribchester, the station's original name, with a southbound rugby special for South Wales on a wintry 21st January 1979. Built in June 1961, D351, as it was originally numbered, ran for less than 20 years before withdrawal in February 1981. (P.J.Fitton)

LANGHO

45. Opened in 1850, the station pictured here with its grand line up of staff in about 1910, lost its passenger service as early as 7th May 1956. (Lens of Sutton)

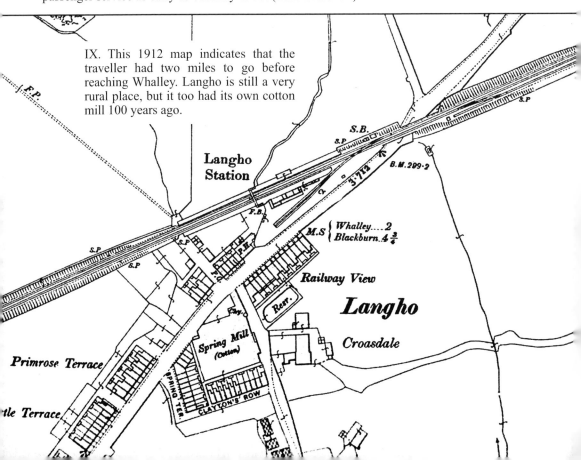

IX. This 1912 map indicates that the traveller had two miles to go before reaching Whalley. Langho is still a very rural place, but it too had its own cotton mill 100 years ago.

46.   With the completion of the Settle-Carlisle Railway and connection to the Blackburn line at Hellifield, the Midland Railway began to run through trains from Scotland to Manchester down the line from 1880. Arriving at Langho, around 1910, is a pair of MR 4-4-0 locomotives with a southbound train. (Lens of Sutton)

47.   During H.C.Casserley's trip along the line on 23rd April 1954, he took this excellent photo from the train showing the up platform and buildings. Of note are the great looking 'Langho' station sign, the ladder in place to inspect the lamps and, strangely, a good number of sleepers! Only two years later the station would be closed. (H.C.Casserley)

48.   The L&Y 24-lever signal box, pictured here, replaced the original 1873 S&F structure. To the right was the entrance to the goods yard that closed on 6th September 1954. An afternoon Hellifield - Liverpool service is pictured in July 1957 headed by ex-LMS class 6P 4-6-0 no. 45607 *Fiji* and behind it can be seen a goods train waiting on the up goods siding. The signal box was closed on 17th September 1962. (K.Roberts)

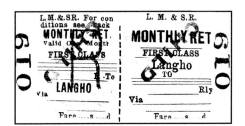

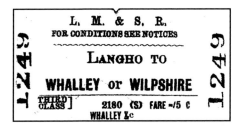

49. By the early 1960s, the station was looking very much worse for wear with its overgrown platforms and decaying buildings. The footbridge survived, but there was no way of using it as the steps had been removed or rotted away. On a wet Lancashire morning a heavy anhydrite train is helped up Whalley Bank, towards Blackburn, by a Standard class 4 locomotive. (K.Roberts)

50. Taking on the 1 in 82 Whalley Bank, locomotive nos. 37198 and 37122 bring the Clitheroe - Gunnie loaded Clyde Cement train past the remains of the old station on 17th July 1986. The Co-Co Type 3 diesels were regular engines for this train, which ran until December 1992. (J.Matthews)

51.   This view is southwards towards Blackburn and work is just underway on the new Langho station on 12th February 1994. Brush Type 4 diesel no. 47820 rushes through with the 'Settle Carlisle Thunderer' special from Stoke-on-Trent to Carlisle. (J.Matthews)

52.   The new station, which opened in May 1994, has staggered platforms. In this photo, taken on 10th November 2010, we see locomotive no. 66561 about to pass the Clitheroe platform with a loaded coal train for Fiddlers Ferry. The mass of Pendle Hill looms large in the distance. (J.Matthews)

SOUTH OF WHALLEY

53. Having just run off the viaduct and starting the climb towards Langho, nos 20025 and 20073 approach Billington crossing with a heavy diverted steel train from Mossend Yard. Captured on film on 11th March 1989, the rear of the train is passing the former Thompson's Siding, which fell away steeply from the Clitheroe bound line just before the viaduct. (J.Matthews)

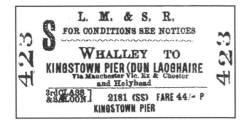

54.   The 48-arch viaduct, known locally as 'Whalley Arches', is the line's most notable engineering feature. Running a length of 679 yards and consisting of seven million bricks it was built in the late 1840s and opened on 20th June 1850. Towering 70ft above the River Calder, it cost around £40,000 to build. Sadly, five people were killed during its construction, three of them on 6th October 1849 when two arches (nos 12 and 13) collapsed. In May 1961, an ex-LMS class 4 2-6-4T engine is seen heading north on the 7.29pm Blackburn - Hellifield service. (K.Roberts)

55.   In an early morning view on 9th June 1984, we see ex-LNER A4 locomotive 4498 *Sir Nigel Gresley* on 'The Clitheronian' special from Clitheroe to York via Blackburn and Manchester Victoria. Organised by Clitheroe Parish Church, the empty coaching stock had earlier run down from Carnforth via Hellifield. Whalley continues to grow, but the trend had started much earlier, with a rise from 1100 people in 1901 to 3905 in 1961. (P.J.Fitton)

ORGANISED RAMBLES

FROM

WILPSHIRE   SETTLE
and
HORTON-IN-RIBBLESDALE

"Limestone Fells of the Craven Country"

*Rambles available for Individuals as well as
Organised Parties*

LEADERS PROVIDED

SPECIAL EXCURSION

TO

WILPSHIRE CLITHEROE HELLIFIELD SETTLE
and HORTON-IN-RIBBLESDALE

Sunday 14th August

FROM	Departure Times	RETURN FARES — THIRD CLASS				
		Wilpshire	Clitheroe	Hellifield	Settle	Horton in Ribblesdale
	am	s d	s d	s d	s d	s d
MANCHESTER VICTORIA	9 43	3 / 6	4 / 9	6 / 3	7 / –	7 / 6
PENDLETON BROAD STREET	9 49	3 / 6	4 / 9	6 / 3	7 / –	7 / 6
BOLTON TRINITY STREET	10 13	2 / 6	3 / 3	5 / 6‡	6 / –	6 / 9
DARWEN	10 40	1 / 6‡	2 / 3	3 / 9	4 / 9	5 / 6
BLACKBURN	10 55	8‡	1 / 9‡	3 / 6‡	3 / 3	5 / –
	am	am	am	am	pm	pm
ARRIVAL TIMES		11 5	11 22	11 49	12 2	12 15
	pm	pm	pm	pm	pm	pm
RETURN TIMES SAME DAY		8 12	7 54	7 30	7 15	7 0

★ Light Refreshments at popular prices will be available on this train

‡—Special cheap day fare.   Available by any train.

The train is due back at Manchester Victoria at 9.43 pm

Children under three years of age free, three years and under fourteen, half-fares.
CONDITIONS OF ISSUE OF EXCURSION AND OTHER TICKETS AT LESS THAN ORDINARY
FARES.
These Tickets are issued subject to the British Transport Commission's published Regulations and Conditions applicable to British Railways exhibited at their Stations or obtainable free of charge at Station Booking Offices.
TICKETS CAN BE OBTAINED IN ADVANCE AT THE STATIONS AND OFFICIAL
RAILWAY AGENCIES.
Further information will be supplied on application to Stations, Official Railway Agencies. or to Mr. T. W. Polding, District Passenger Manager, L.M.R., Hunts Bank, Manchester, 3. Tel. BLA 3456   Ext 587

July, 1955   XB/HD   BR 35001

BRITISH RAILWAYS

Hills Printers Chorley.,   E676/HD

X.   Here is a 1955 notice for a rambler's excursion to the Ribble Valley, Settle and Horton-in-Ribblesdale. This was an early version of the DalesRail trains that continue to run in 2016. Starting out from Manchester Victoria at 9.43am, the special train would return there exactly 12 hours later.

56.   In the year 1296, a group of Cistercian monks arrived from Stanlow in Cheshire and soon laid the first stone for Whalley Abbey. It was completed some 150 years later in 1450 and now the ruins are an important part of the village's history, as well as a visitor attraction. On 3rd March 1995, the 08.16 Clitheroe to Manchester service heads south, about to cross over one of the specially-styled arches made to blend in with the nearby Abbey. (J.Matthews)

57.   In November 2001, the historic viaduct was newly waterproofed in nine days at a cost of £2 million. All the old jointed track and ballast were removed and, after the waterproofing membrane was laid, as we see here, new long-welded track and steel sleepers were put in place. (K.Roberts)

58.   On 28th December 2002, a year or so after the new waterproofing, the viaduct looks in good shape as a Birmingham to Carlisle special runs north in the hands of Deltic no. 9016 *Gordon Highlander* in its distinctive purple 'Porterbrook' livery.   (J.Matthews)

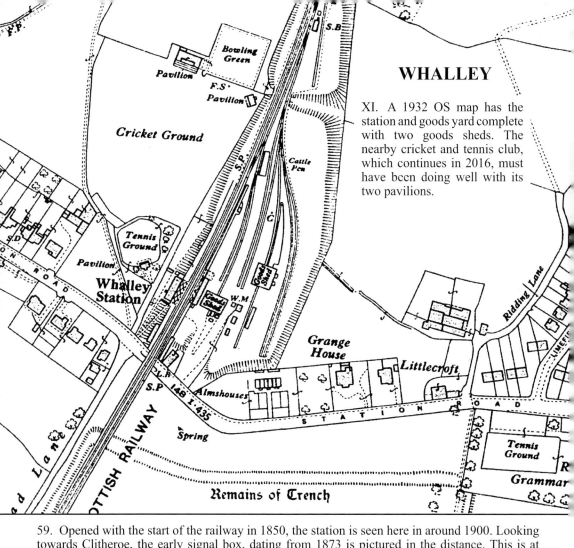

WHALLEY

XI. A 1932 OS map has the station and goods yard complete with two goods sheds. The nearby cricket and tennis club, which continues in 2016, must have been doing well with its two pavilions.

59. Opened with the start of the railway in 1850, the station is seen here in around 1900. Looking towards Clitheroe, the early signal box, dating from 1873 is pictured in the distance. This is at the end of the Blackburn platform and guards the entrance to the goods yard that lay to the right. (B.Haworth coll.)

60. Arriving at Whalley in the late 1950s is a class 4 2-6-0 locomotive with a local service from Blackburn to Hellifield. The station closed for passengers on 10th September 1962. (SLS)

61. Four years after closure, the station is looking neglected as the banking engine runs onto the back of a heavy up freight train. The banker would have run out of the loop next to the signal box and was needed to assist the train up the 1 in 82 bank from the line's lowest point to Wilpshire. To the left is the closed goods yard, which, in its heyday, had a 5-ton crane and could handle anything from general goods to livestock and horseboxes. The yard outlived the passenger service by around 18 months, closing on 23rd March 1964. (K.Roberts)

62. The original Saxby and Farmer 20-lever signal box of 1873 was replaced in 1912 by the L&Y one you see here in February 1975. Heading south with a diverted Glasgow - Birmingham train is no. 47269. Time was running out for the splendid looking box, which was closed on 10th November 1974. (P.J.Fitton)

63. By the early 1980s the northbound platform building still survived, although in a terrible state of repair; even the attempt to protect the roof was now in tatters. On 4th April 1981, a two-car diesel unit runs into the sorry-looking former station with a 'DalesRail' service to Carlisle. (J.Matthews)

64. The new Whalley station received its first train on 29th May 1994, some 32 years after the regular service was withdrawn. The platform building to the left survived to see better days and, now privately owned, it has seen use by various commercial firms. The 10.58 Clitheroe - Shaw train, in the form of no. 150205, arrives on 28th August 1995. Patronage from Whalley had risen to over 90,000 passengers per year by 2013. (J.Matthews)

CALDERSTONES BRANCH

65. The short branch line from Barrow Sidings, just north of Whalley, was built in 1909 to bring in construction materials for the Lancashire Asylums Board's new hospital at Calderstones. Before it could be used as planned, World War I broke out and it was offered to the War Office to treat injured soldiers, being known as Queen Mary's Military Hospital from 1915 to 1920. The ambulance train platforms are pictured in around 1916. (B.Haworth coll.)

XII. A 6ins map has the track of the future Calderstones Hospital branch line in 1914. Work has still to start on the soon to be called 'Queen Mary's Military Hospital'.

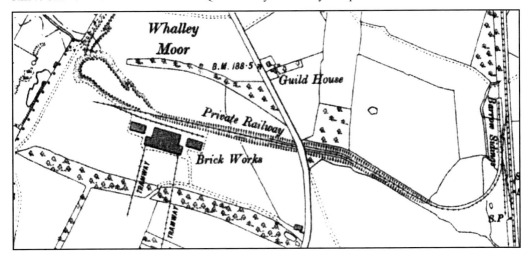

66. On 6th May 1915, the first train of injured soldiers arrived from Southampton. Very few photos survive of the line's operation, although here we can see an excellent artist's sketch, capturing the arrival of a World War I train complete with Red Cross sign and 'GCR' lettering on the near coach. (B.Haworth coll.)

XIII. A later map, this time from 1932, clearly shows the larger radius curve of the line away from Barrow Sidings to accommodate the WWI ambulance trains. The extent of the Institution, as it was called here, is obvious with its own club, football ground, schools and church.

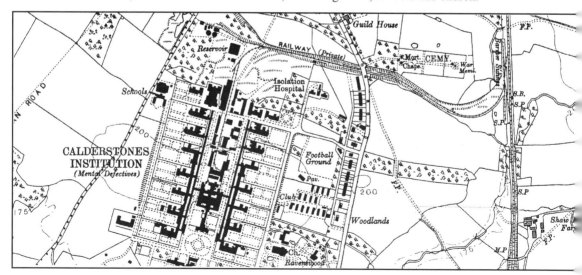

67. Early locomotives, *The Whalley* and *The Thornhill*, worked the line until the arrival of an 0-4-0 fireless engine built by Andrew Barclay in 1925. The engine, pictured outside the engine shed in the mid-1940s, operated until the end of traffic in 1949. (B.Haworth coll.)

68. One of the last features of the railway to survive was the section of trackbed that ran under the B6246 road to Mitton, just north of Whalley. Due to heavy road traffic, the bridge developed serious cracks in the brickwork and, by 2000, was filled in. (B.Haworth coll.)

SOUTH OF CLITHEROE

69.   Overlooked by the 12th Century keep of Clitheroe Castle is the Low Moor Sidings signal box and crossing. Built in 1873, and receiving a new L&Y frame of 28 levers in 1892, the box was soon to meet an untimely end. We see it here in February 1976 being passed by a diverted southbound Inter-City service of mixed Mk.1 and Mk.2 stock, headed by English Electric Co-Co locomotive no. 50040, later named *Leviathan*. (P.J.Fitton)

70.   A scene of total devastation at Low Moor Crossing is pictured on 9th November 1976, after a southbound freight had derailed and literally wiped out the signal box. In this poignant image, we see the rescue gang starting the job of repairing the railway. They are ably assisted by the steam crane, probably from Springs Branch, Wigan, and no. 40137, a long-time Carlisle-based engine. The signalman escaped with his life and just a few scratches! (P.J.Fitton)

71. In the far middle distance is the cement works, while a little nearer can be seen Low Moor level crossing, controlled from Horrocksford box since July 1979. Low Moor signal box had controlled a host of goods sidings, south of Clitheroe, but by the time of this image, in September 1981, all were long gone. Split headcode loco no. 40127 was built in December 1960 and after a relatively short life of less than 22 years was withdrawn on the 14th February 1982. The former D327, that had spent a number of years allocated to Wigan Springs Branch shed, is seen with a train of Presflos from Ribblesdale Cement, heading for Blackburn. (T.Heavyside)

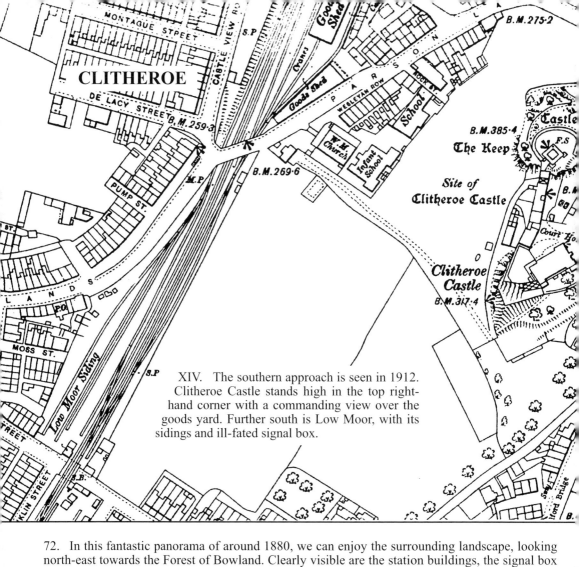

XIV. The southern approach is seen in 1912. Clitheroe Castle stands high in the top right-hand corner with a commanding view over the goods yard. Further south is Low Moor, with its sidings and ill-fated signal box.

72. In this fantastic panorama of around 1880, we can enjoy the surrounding landscape, looking north-east towards the Forest of Bowland. Clearly visible are the station buildings, the signal box in the bottom left corner, dating from 1873, and, between them, the goods yard. From behind the box runs the Clitheroe Corporation Gas Works line and sidings. (B.Haworth coll.)

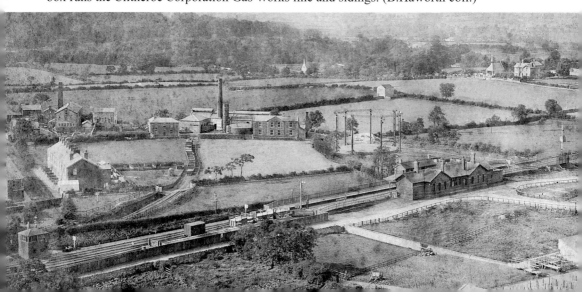

73. We now have a view from an early postcard in L&Y days, around 1900. The milk carts and horses are gathered before departing with their deliveries. Further back we see a busy goods yard overlooked by the signal box; this had opened in 1873 with a 23-lever S&F frame. It was in operation for almost 100 years, closing in 1970, by which time a 20-lever L&Y frame had been installed. The footbridge and water tower are seen at the end of the station. At this time, the town had a population of 11,414 that rose by less than 1000 in 1961. (P.Laming coll.)

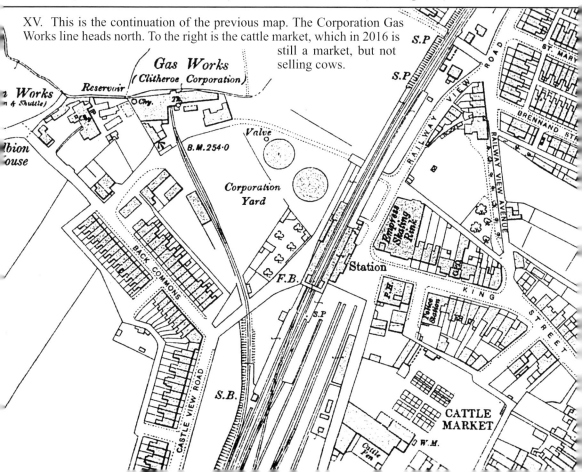

XV. This is the continuation of the previous map. The Corporation Gas Works line heads north. To the right is the cattle market, which in 2016 is still a market, but not selling cows.

74. The station is seen, looking south in the mid-1950s. An ex-LMS 2P 4-4-0 engine waits to continue with a local service to Hellifield, while a number of travellers have left the train and head for home. (SLS)

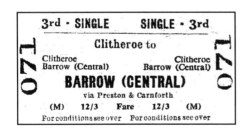

75. The town's first station opened in 1850 but was replaced by one on the present site in 1893. After the end of regular passenger services the station fell into disrepair, although in this photo of 1960 all seems in good shape. The building was eventually bought by brewers Daniel Thwaites and after much restoration it was reopened in 1994 as an art gallery and visitors centre. For the three-wheeler enthusiasts, a Bond mini car, complete with Villiers two-stroke engine is on the far left. (K.Roberts)

76. Besides a number of private sidings serving the NW Gas Board and the grandly named Trinidad Mastic Supply, Clitheroe had an extensive goods yard. Equipped with a 10-ton crane, the yard could handle any kind of traffic, from livestock to general merchandise, but was closed on 1st September 1969. This view, looking north, shows the yard in January 1961 being shunted by an ex-LMS 2-6-0 loco; later the site was used for a supermarket and car park. (K.Roberts)

77. A feature of the station was the grand footbridge at its southern end. Posing below it is ex-LMS 4-6-0 class 5 no. 45233 on a Blackburn-bound train, viewed here on 4th November 1961, just 10 months before closure. Built in August 1936, no. 45233 was mainly a Manchester locomotive, spending 1938-64 at Newton Heath before being moved to Trafford Park. It was withdrawn in May 1966. (G.W.Morrison)

78. Proving that Clitheronians are some of the most enthusiastic railway people in the world, hundreds of townsfolk, including the town crier, to the left, welcome no. 40198 heading a northbound freight for Carlisle Yard on 8th April 1978. Seriously though, the crowd had gathered to greet the first Ribble Valley 'DalesRail' train, 16 years after the passenger service finished on 10th September 1962. The DMU, seen in picture 40, would follow the goods train and pull up at the clearly visible, but incomplete, new platform. (P.J.Fitton)

79. The new station, six months after opening, sees a Santa Special train arrive from Preston on 26th November 1994. On the new northbound platform, passengers leave for a visit to the town's shops, while, to the right, the old station building lives on as an art gallery and visitors centre. (J.Matthews)

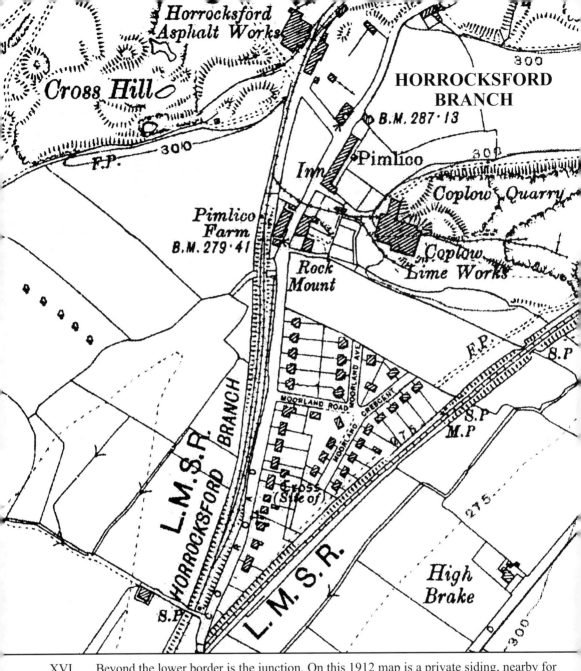

XVI.   Beyond the lower border is the junction. On this 1912 map is a private siding, nearby for exchange purposes. The abundance of limestone around Clitheroe is well-known and even in 2016 provides a good living for many workers at Castle Cement.

80. On 7th March 1976, a Brush Type 4 brings a Euston - Glasgow service past the 1873 signal box and through the junction. The prominent gasholder in the distance is no longer standing. (P.J.Fitton)

81. Just into the branch line it soon becomes double track and remains so for much of its length; just over half a mile. Over the years, trains have arrived at Horrocksford from both the north and south. It was from the latter, via Blackburn, that this Saturday extra working arrived from Mossend. On the wet morning of 19th March 1988, locos nos 37677 and 37681 are seen on the branch facing the junction. (J.Matthews)

82. Around halfway along the branch line to Castle Cement, the vegetation closes in as the 'Chopper Topper' railtour heads back towards the junction on 31st May 2014. The special, that brought unusual motive power to this part of the world, had started from Crewe and on its journey negotiated the new Todmorden Curve. (J.Matthews)

83.   Having crossed the minor road for West Bradford, here we see the surviving Type 1 Clayton heading a train of empty PCA wagons into the works. The Bo-Bo loco, numbered D8568 in its short time on BR metals, was one of 117 built from 1962, but all had been withdrawn by December 1971. Pictured on 16th September 1981, the engine was to go into preservation after leaving the Ribblesdale Cement Works, as it was called in those days. (T.Heavyside)

84.   While cement trains to Scotland restarted in March 2008, the earlier flows north of the border and to Newcastle ceased on 18th December 1992. In the early 1990s, Castle Cement was informed by the rail company of the time that the train to Newcastle was uneconomic and cancelled it. Although Castle Cement tried their best to reverse this, the cement traffic to Clyde was also lost, putting 250,000 tons of cement onto the roads! The picture shows the works' shunters and PCA wagons on the day before the last train in December 1992. Hanson, now the site's owners, has overseen a resurgence in rail traffic with daily trains to Mossend and Avonmouth. (P.J.Fitton)

85.   Although the main rail traffic on the branch was cement, there were also regular coal trains from various locations like Redcar, Immingham and the Yorkshire coalfields. On 9th April 1997, we have a view well inside the works as no. 37680 waits with the empties for Healey Mills Yard. (J.Matthews)

86.   We are now at the quarry face, located between the works and Chatburn, in 1950. A Ruston Bucyrus electric loading shovel, note the cable, fills the waiting Ribble Cement wagons with limestone. From there, the load would be taken to the cement works crusher to start the production process. (P.del Strother)

NORTH OF CLITHEROE

87. After the trip up the branch line we are now back on the main line at Horrocksford. As mentioned earlier, the very first 'DalesRail' along the Ribble Valley has just called at Clitheroe and now heads north for Carlisle on 8th April 1978. Based on the Ramblers Excusions of yesteryear, these trains were a link between Lancashire and the Settle-Carlisle line. Running on Saturdays or Sundays they started out from a number of places including Manchester and Blackpool. The box was still open in 2016. It had its original 19-lever frame replaced in 1928 by a 12-lever L&Y type. (P.J.Fitton)

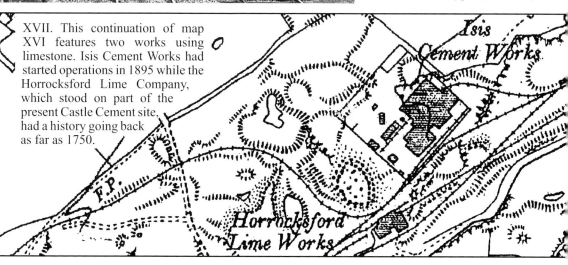

XVII. This continuation of map XVI features two works using limestone. Isis Cement Works had started operations in 1895 while the Horrocksford Lime Company, which stood on part of the present Castle Cement site, had a history going back as far as 1750.

88. Between Clitheroe and Chatburn were extensive lime quarries, kilns and cement works. Looking north, on the left was Bankfield while, to the right, was Bellmanpark, with a tramway connection to its own quarry. A further 1550-yard mineral line to Salt Hill Quarry was added in 1898 and it ran into Bellmanpark sidings. The signal box at Bankfield Sidings, that controlled all this activity, can be seen middle left and lasted until 1st February 1966. The end of production was around 1960. (M.Seddon)

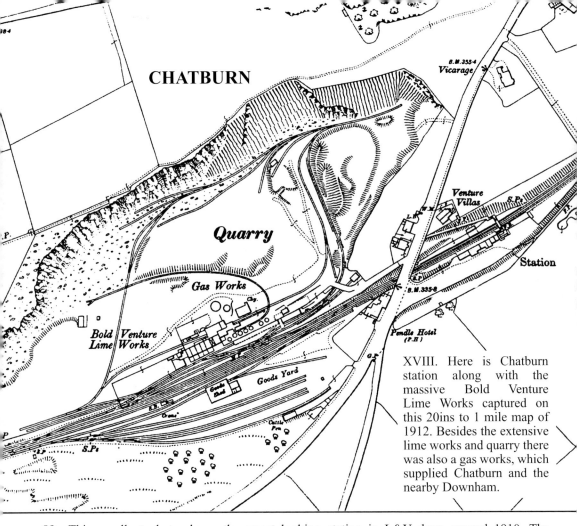

CHATBURN

Quarry

Gas Works

Bold Venture Lime Works

Goods Yard

Vicarage

Venture Villas

Station

Pendle Hotel (P.H)

XVIII. Here is Chatburn station along with the massive Bold Venture Lime Works captured on this 20ins to 1 mile map of 1912. Besides the extensive lime works and quarry there was also a gas works, which supplied Chatburn and the nearby Downham.

89. This excellent photo shows the smart looking station in L&Y days, around 1910. The station's staff is out in force and even spilling onto the tracks! A lone passenger arrives through the gate to the right, whilst on close inspection, we see the information board, to his right, has a 'MIDLAND' heading. The population of the town, which stands 400ft above sea level, was 772 in 1901. (B.Haworth coll.)

90. The station canopy and footbridge are visible through the road bridge in the distance as class 4F no. 44462 arrives at Chatburn goods yard in 1961. The pickup freight's loco would shunt the yard and collect any empties from the goods shed, the roof of which can be seen above the condemned wagon on the right. The engine pictured had been built at Horwich in 1928 and was in service until being withdrawn from Workington in November 1965. (K.Roberts)

91. In 1962, only a matter of months before closure on 10th September, class 4MT 2-6-0 no. 76080 conjures up an almost ghostly scene having arrived with a Hellifield - Blackburn local train. One of 115 of the class, 76080 was built as late as 1957 and lasted only 10 years before being withdrawn from Wigan depot in the last month of 1967. (P.J.Fitton)

92. In the foreground we find the former Hellifield platform, although the stone slab edgings have been broken up. In March 1983, passing through a very wet station scene we see a class 25 heading north on a Sunday engineering train. (J.Matthews)

Lancashire&Yorkshire Railway

ONE DOG (Accompanied) (by Passenger)

CHATBURN To

On
the Rly.

Via

PAID s. d.

This Ticket is available for a Single journey only and must be given up at Destination Station

See conditions on back

274

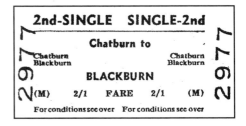

2nd-SINGLE   SINGLE-2nd

Chatburn to

Chatburn
Blackburn

Chatburn
Blackburn

BLACKBURN

(M)   2/1   FARE   2/1   (M)

For conditions see over   For conditions see over

2977

2977

93.   The first station at Chatburn opened in 1850 and was the terminus of the line until a new station was opened 100 yards further north in 1876. A good part of the station remains in use in 2016. On 1st May 1988, no. 47604 passes the still intact Blackburn platform and building with a diverted Glasgow - London Euston service. (T.Heavyside)

94.   The end of goods traffic at Chatburn station came on 23rd March 1964. Prior to that, virtually all types of goods were handled with the help of the 5-ton crane and impressive goods shed. The well maintained building still looks fit for its original purpose some 50 years after closure, pictured here in April 2014. (J.Matthews)

NORTH OF CHATBURN

95.   Between Chatburn and Rimington this attractive viaduct takes the line high over Ings Beck, which runs on into the River Ribble. On 25th March 1995, ex-BR 4-6-2 no. 70000 *Britannia* runs tender first on its way from Keighley to Lostock Hall. (J.Matthews)

96.   Now we have a wide view of the North Lancashire landscape looking back towards Clitheroe and the cement works. On 1st January 2000, a Virgin HST heads south over the viaduct with a diverted Edinburgh to Bournemouth service. Close by is the small village of Downham sitting in the shadow of Pendle Hill. This timeless location was used for the filming of the 1961 film *'Whistle Down The Wind'* and later, the BBC series *'Born and Bred'*. (J.Matthews)

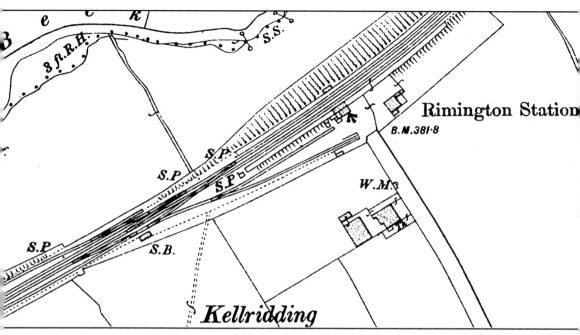

XIX.   When looking for a truly rural railway station, you would have had to look no further than Rimington, as seen in this map of 1908. Swanside Beck runs a little north of the line making its way to the Ribble.

97.   Serving a tiny rural community, the station was opened in 1872. It was an early casualty with the passenger service ceasing on 7th July 1958. Looking north, a year or so later, what appears to be a special working is about to run through the already overgrown platforms. (SLS)

98.   An early 1960s' view is from the signal box and is of a class 5MT 2-6-0 rushing north through the station with an express freight. The goods yard, to the right, was closed on 7th July 1958, alongwith the passenger station. The box had opened in 1879, being fitted with a 17-lever frame, and it continued in business until September 1962. (K.Roberts)

99.   Again, seen from the location of the former signal box, this May 1986 photograph shows us no. 47555 *The Commonwealth Spirit* on the diverted 07.05 Glasgow - Euston InterCity train. It is passing the remains of the up platform, as the surviving station house appears to be receiving a delivery of concrete over to the right. (J.Matthews)

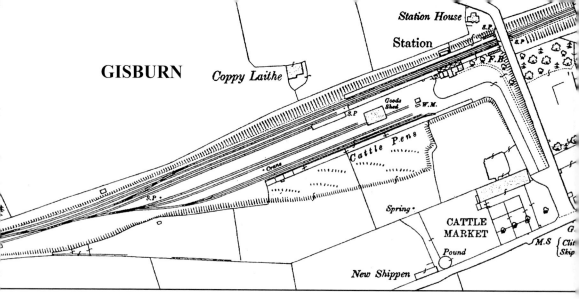

XX. The 20ins to 1 mile map from 1909 shows the line just before it disappears into the tunnel in the top right-hand corner. An extensive goods yard with cattle pens was provided and a little south is the cattle market, which is still alive in 2016. The A59 trunk road cuts through the lower half of the map and the centre of Gisburn, bringing a continuous flow of heavy traffic to this lovely historic village. There was no ring road nor station for Gisburn in 2016.

100. At the time of this photo, around 1890, Gisburn was in the West Riding of Yorkshire, but today it is part of Lancashire. A perfect setting, then, for some of the station staff to pose against an L&Y Railway adorned backdrop. (B.Haworth coll.)

101. Opened by the L&Y Railway on 2nd June 1879, the station was for a short time the terminus of the line before the full opening to Hellifield on 1st June 1880. This 1907 northward view shows the station, with the grand station masters house high to the left. (P.Laming)

102. Heading north through the station in the late 1950s is class 5MT 4-6-0 no. 44884 with a down goods train that includes fuel tanks. To the left, seen above the platform canopy, is the goods yard complete with a 5 ton crane and facilities to handle general traffic and livestock. Closure of the goods yard came on 23rd March 1964. The engine, built in 1945, nearly saw out the end of steam on BR, being withdrawn from Newton Heath (26A) on 30th June 1968. (K.Roberts)

103.   The last regular passenger train had called on 10th September 1962, although a large crowd were out in force on 23rd May 1964 to see no. 72007 *Clan Mackintosh*. The near 87-ton class 6P5F 4-6-2 engine, withdrawn in December 1965 after just 13 years service, was in charge of the RCTS 'Ribble Lune Railtour' from Preston to Heysham. (P.J.Fitton)

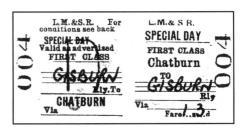

104.   Set in the rural North Lancashire landscape, Gisburn signal box is pictured on 10th March 1974. Built in 1879 as a 21-lever Saxby and Farmer type 9 box, it was closed on 18th March 1981, although the story didn't end there! (P.J.Fitton)

105.   On closure, the signal box was bought by a local businessman and saved from demolition at the last minute. It is still standing in 2016, although not in the best of condition. Here on 1st August 1990, a Hellifield to Bolton weed killer train passes south. Leading the train is Type 1 Bo-Bo no. 20902 *Lorna* partnered by fellow class member no. 20905 *Iona* at the rear. (J.Matthews)

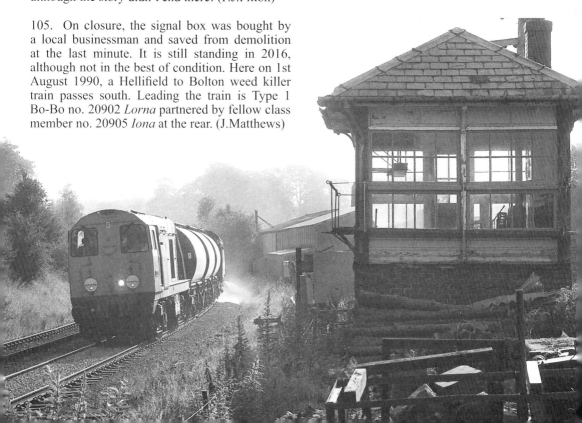

106. Just north of the station is the 156-yard Gisburn Tunnel that was insisted on by the then landowner, Lord Ribblesdale, to hide the railway from the view of his stately home at nearby Gisburne Park. At the ornamental south portal of the tunnel, we have a great view of ex-LNER A4 4-6-2 loco no. 4498 *Sir Nigel Gresley* heading the SLOA special, 'The Mancunian', on 3rd May 1980. The special had started at Crewe before running via Manchester, Woodhead, Leeds, Carnforth and Hellifield. The locomotive, built in 1937 and withdrawn from Aberdeen Ferryhill on 1st February 1966, had taken over the train when it reversed at Carnforth for the southbound leg of the tour. (P.J.Fitton)

107.   Gisburn Tunnel or 'covered way' as it was referred to in the early days, runs beneath the private road to Gisburne Park House, now a hospital. Top left, we can see the very ornate gatehouse or lodge as Type 4 1Co-Co1 loco no. 40030 runs north out of the tunnel. The train is a 'Radio Blackburn' special, heading for Keighley via Hellifield on 2nd April 1977. (P.J.Fitton)

108.   On leaving the tunnel the line soon runs over Stock Beck, crossed by an attractive eight arch, 500ft-long viaduct. On 20th February 1981, no. 40012 rushes north with a morning Bescot Yard to Carlisle Yard mixed goods. (J.Matthews)

109.   After a short level stretch through Gisburn, the line climbs the 1 in 105 bank towards the summit at Newsholme. This panorama shows us the distant, but unmistakable 1830ft-high Pendle Hill. Known for its links with the witch trials of 1612, this seven mile-wide hill is never out of sight from Wilpshire Tunnel to Hellifield. On the morning of 23rd September 2003, no. 56060 brings a Crewe Basford Hall to Carlisle engineers train towards the summit. (J.Matthews)

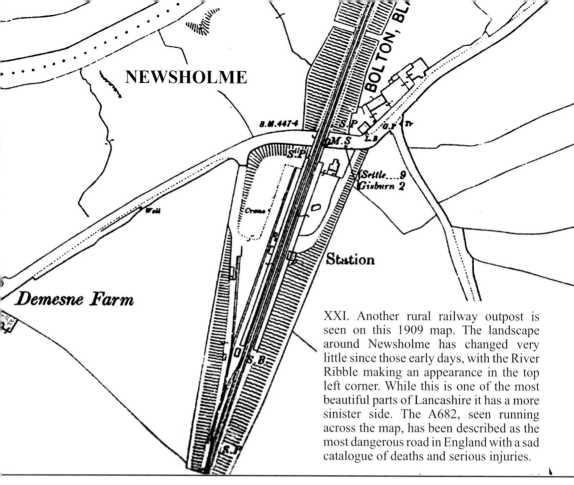

NEWSHOLME

BOLTON, BL

Demesne Farm

B.M.447·4

S P

O.F Tr

L.B

M.S

S.P

Srttle....9
Gisburn 2

Well

Crane

Station

S.B.

S.J.

XXI. Another rural railway outpost is seen on this 1909 map. The landscape around Newsholme has changed very little since those early days, with the River Ribble making an appearance in the top left corner. While this is one of the most beautiful parts of Lancashire it has a more sinister side. The A682, seen running across the map, has been described as the most dangerous road in England with a sad catalogue of deaths and serious injuries.

110.   The search for old photographs proved as difficult to find as was the station for passengers, it being many miles from civilisation, except for the odd farm or two. The station saw early closure of all services on 6th August 1957. The station house, just visible behind the train, survives in private hands, while the small goods yard is still clearly picked out behind the wooden huts to the left. No. 47530 passes through the former station in heavy rain on 18th March 1989, heading the 07.20 Glasgow - Poole train. (J.Matthews)

111.   Also well known as the Ribble Valley Line, the Blackburn - Hellifield railway is never far from the River Ribble. This begins its journey close to the Ribblehead Viaduct and runs 75 miles through North Yorkshire and Lancashire into the Irish Sea at Preston. At Nappa, two miles south of Hellifield, the river is just 200 yards down to the right, as 4F 0-6-0 no. 44460 brings a morning Blackburn - Hellifield train north in the late 1950s. (K.Roberts)

112.   At the northern end of the line there were extensive sidings and even an engine shed in the early days. All were long gone in this great image of 21st August 1980, as locos no. 40163 and no. 40179 run onto the Blackburn line with a great looking mixed goods for Bescot Yard. (J.S. Whiteley)

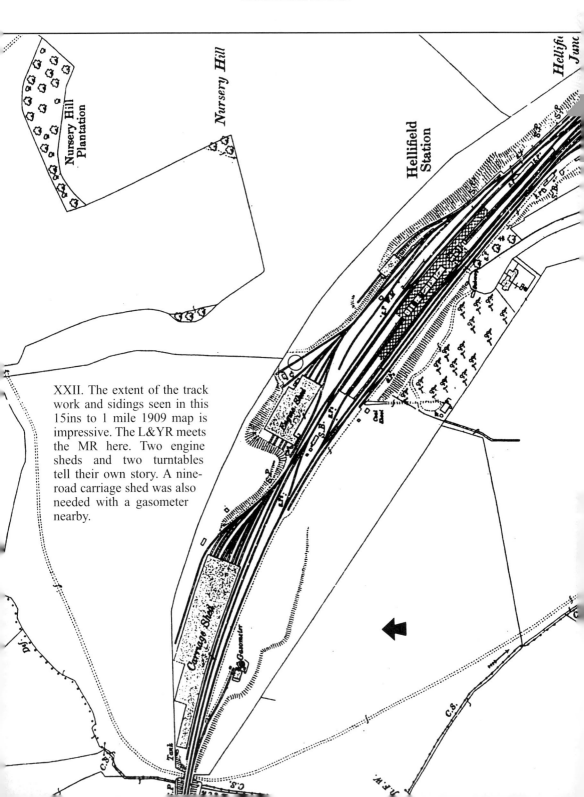

Nursery Hill Plantation

Nursery Hill

Hellifield Station

Hellifield Junc

XXII. The extent of the track work and sidings seen in this 15ins to 1 mile 1909 map is impressive. The L&YR meets the MR here. Two engine sheds and two turntables tell their own story. A nine-road carriage shed was also needed with a gasometer nearby.

Engine Shed

Carriage Shed

Gasometer

Tank

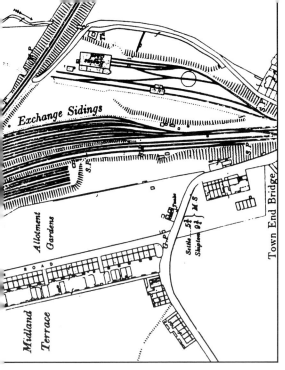

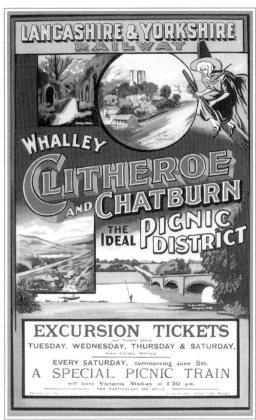

113.   At the northbound platform, in around 1900, a pair of 4-4-0 Midland Railway engines prepare to depart with a 'Scotch Express', that had probably run up the Ribble Valley from Manchester. (P.Laming coll.)

114.   Opened in 1880, the grand MR station was preceded by a much smaller one, sited a little further south and built in 1849 by the 'Little North Western Railway'. Looking from the north, we see the Hellifield up platform for Skipton and Leeds trains in around 1900. Of interest are the large stack of baskets, possibly for small livestock and the 'Refreshments Third Class' sign. Not sure if that was for third class food or not! (P.Laming coll.)

115.   In the station's south bay on 28th May 1949, a class 3 ex-LMS 2-6-2T waits to depart with a train for the Ribble Valley and Blackburn. Based at Hellifield shed for a time and still carrying its LMS number 21, it was soon to become no. 40021 and continue in service until 12th September 1959. (H.C.Casserley.)

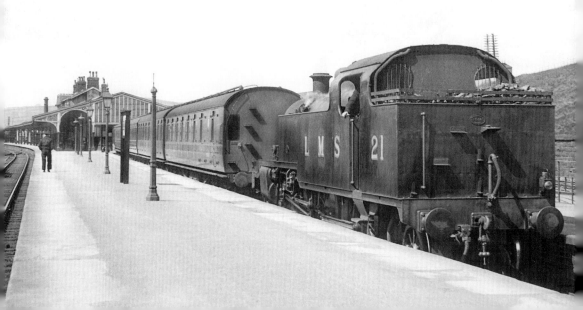

116. At the junction with the line to Blackburn, the South Junction box stands tall as a Leeds - Morecambe service rushes through, led by no. 45505, *The Royal Army Ordnance Corps*. To the right is the northern end of the Ribble Valley route, with a good array of signals, as a 2-6-4T engine propels a short van train into the station in the Spring of 1962. Further down the line, to the right, would have stood Hellifield Goods Yard signal box, which closed in late 1957. (M.Chapman)

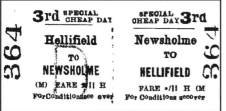

117. We are now at the north end of the station on 1st June 1963. The Midland Railway signal box is pictured at the end of the Carlisle facing bay, while to the right is the impressive Hellifield steam shed. (H.C.Casserley)

↓ 118. We now catch a glimpse inside the steam shed, just two weeks before its closure on 17th June 1963. The light filters through the shed roof to highlight class 4F 0-6-0 no. 44479 from Lower Darwen, class 4 2-6-4T no. 42492 off Newton Heath and, on the right, 4-6-0 class 6P5F loco no. 45602 *British Honduras*, a Leeds Holbeck engine. After its closure to steam, the depot was used to store locomotives claimed for the National Collection pending moves to suitable collections. (H.C.Casserley.)

119.   South Junction on 3rd January 1965 and glorious weather for the first ever West Coast Main Line diversions via the S&C. Three days into the New Year and Type 4 diesel loco no. D295 brings the diverted up 'Royal Scot' onto the Blackburn line. Renumbered no. 40095 on 31st December 1973, it was withdrawn from service in September 1981. (P.J.Fitton)

120. To round off our journey, we have a view of the RCTS 'Rebuilt Scot Commemorative Railtour' that ran on 13th February 1965 from Crewe to Carlisle. After running via Wigan and Chorley, the special headed for Blackburn, before taking the Clitheroe line. After a stop, class 7P 4-6-0 loco no. 46115 *Scots Guardsman* restarts the train for the S&C passing the old shed and a throng of photographers. (P.J.Fitton)

MP Middleton Press
EVOLVING THE ULTIMATE RAIL ENCYCLOPEDIA

Easebourne Midhurst GU29 9AZ. Tel:01730 813169

www.middletonpress.co.uk   email:info@middletonpress.co.uk
A-978 0 906520   B- 978 1 873793   C- 978 1 901706   D-978 1 904474
E- 978 1 906008   F- 978 1 908174